Material Matters
Plastics

Terry Jennings

Chrysalis Education

Distributed in the United States by
Smart Apple Media
1980 Lookout Drive
North Mankato, MN 56003

Copyright © Chrysalis Books PLC 2003

ISBN 1-93233-303-7

The Library of Congress control number 2003102411

Editorial Manager: Joyce Bentley
Series Editor: Sarah Nunn
Design: Stonecastle Graphics Ltd
Picture Researcher: Paul Turner

Printed in China

10 9 8 7 6 5 4 3 2 1

Picture credits:
Roddy Paine Photographic Studios: pages 8 (left), 10, 12-13, 14-15, 16 (below), 17 (top), 19, 20-21, 23,
24, 25 (below), 28-29.
Spectrum Colour Library: pages 6-7.
Stonecastle Graphics: pages 5, 26.
Transco: page 18.

contents

Plastics everywhere 4

How are plastics made? 6

The main kinds of plastic 8

Shaping plastics 10

Plastic toys 12

Plastics for building 14

Plastics and electricity 16

Plastic pipes 18

Plastics and our food 20

Plastic clothes 22

Plastics keep us safe 24

Getting rid of waste plastic 26

Do it yourself 28

Glossary 30

Index 32

plastics everywhere

You can see **plastics** almost everywhere. There are plastics in your home and at school.

The plastic called Teflon is very slippery. It is used to coat the surface of frying pans so that the food does not stick.

Plastics are often used instead of metals, wood, and glass. Plastics are light and they do not **rust** or **rot**. You can see through some plastics, while many are difficult to break. Some plastics are hard and stiff, others are soft and bendy.

You probably have toys and games made from plastic.

How are plastics made?

Plastics are **manufactured materials**. They are made in a factory. The first plastics were made from wood. Some plastics are still made from wood or coal. But most are made from **chemicals** that come from oil. Plastics are not colored at first, so a **dye** is added to color them.

This factory makes plastics.

These new plastic bottles will soon be ready to leave the factory.

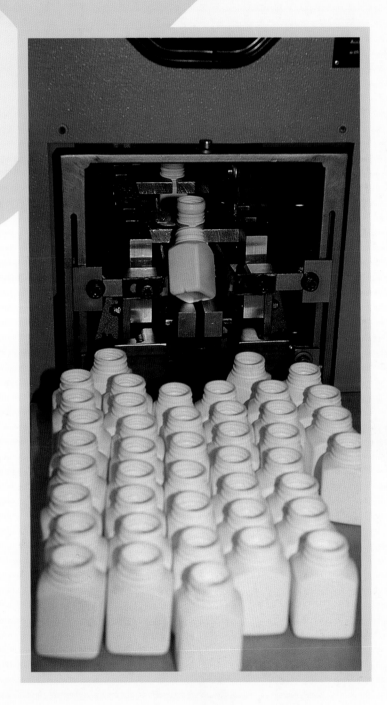

The first plastics were made over 150 years ago. They caught fire easily and so were not used very much.

7

The main kinds of plastic

There are two main groups of plastics. Some, such as those used to make telephones and radios, can only be heated and shaped once. They cannot then be made into new shapes.

These plastics can be heated and shaped only once.

These plastics can be melted and shaped many times.

The first plastic to be used a lot was called Bakelite. Early in the 20th century it was used to make radios and telephones.

Some other plastics, such as **polyethylene** or **polystyrene**, can be **melted** again and again. They can be made into a new shape each time.

shaping plastics

Plastics leave the factory as small white pellets. These are then melted and shaped to form bags or bottles. Some are rolled flat to make floor tiles.

This is what most plastics look like when they leave the factory.

Buckets, bowls, and boxes are usually shaped by squirting the plastic into a shape, called a **mold**.

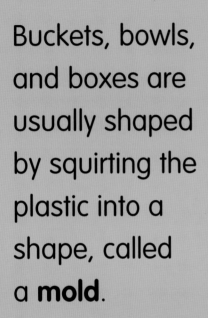

Polyethylene, a common plastic, was first made in the 1930s.

Even large plastic objects, like this bin, can be made using a mold.

Plastic toys

Many plastic toys are made in molds. If toy bricks are being made, the mold is the shape of the brick.

Toy bricks like these are made in a mold.

The world's tallest structure made from toy bricks was built in Taiwan. It was a pyramid more than 80 feet high.

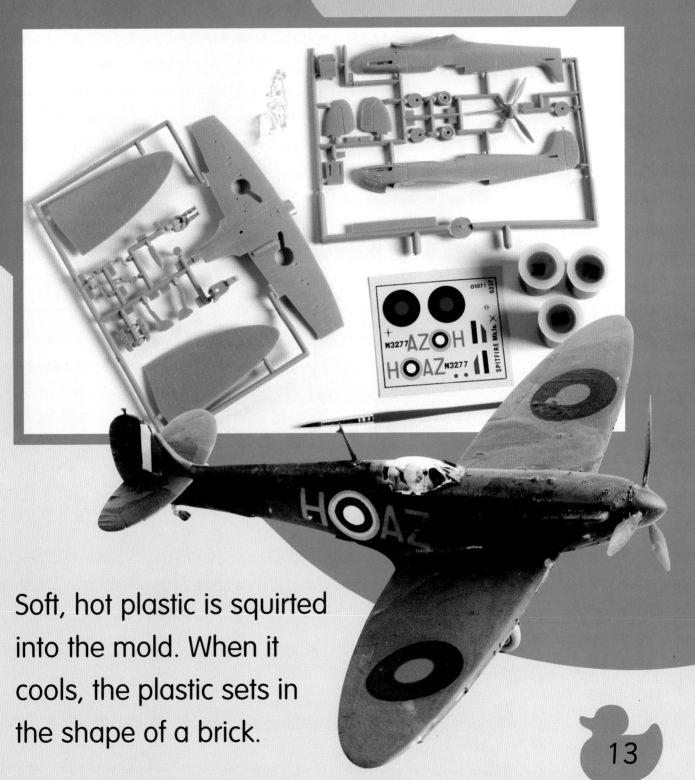

The parts of this plastic model aircraft were made in a mold.

Soft, hot plastic is squirted into the mold. When it cools, the plastic sets in the shape of a brick.

plastics for building

Many doors, window frames, and pipes are made from plastic. Plastic is used because it does not rust or rot, and does not have to be painted.

Plastic doors and windows are easy to keep clean and last for a long time.

The pipes that take rainwater from the roofs of buildings are now made of plastic. They used to be made of iron.

The roofs of many **conservatories** are made of plastic. This is because the plastic material is light and you can see through it. It will not break like glass might.

plastics and electricity

Plastic is used to cover electrical wires, plugs, and sockets. Electricity cannot pass through most plastics, so plastics help to keep us safe.

The plastic covering on this wire and these fuses stops electricity reaching us.

NEVER touch electric sockets, plugs, or wires.

Many things that use electricity have a plastic covering.

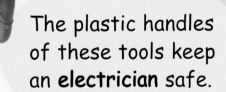

The plastic handles of these tools keep an **electrician** safe.

17

Plastic pipes

Plastic is now used for many pipes instead of metals such as iron, **lead**, or **copper**.

Plastic pipes, like this gas pipe, are strong, light, and bend easily.

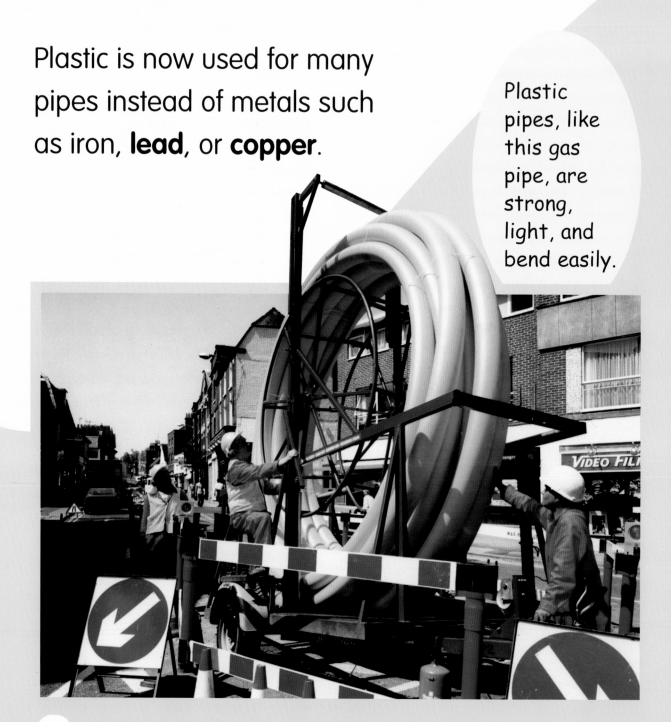

The large pipes that carry water and gas under the streets are made of plastic. Some of the water pipes inside our homes are also made of plastic.

Plastic water pipes come in many different shapes and sizes.

plastics and our food

Some plastics help to keep our food fresh for longer. Plastic bags stop bread from drying out. Polystyrene boxes are used to keep burgers hot.

Polystyrene keeps food and drinks warm and stops us from burning our fingers.

The sides of a refrigerator also contain polystyrene. This helps to keep heat out of the refrigerator, so that our food stays cool.

Polystyrene can be made into a very light foam. It is used to pack around fragile equipment.

The plastic inside a refrigerator is easy to clean. It also helps to keep our food cool.

plastic clothes

Some plastics can be made into fine **fibers**. These fibers are stronger than wool or cotton. If they are woven into cloth, the cloth is often **waterproof** and warm.

This girl's winter clothes are made of plastic materials. They keep her warm and dry.

Plastic boots are waterproof.

Sometimes plastic fibers are mixed with wool or cotton to make clothes. The plastic fibers make the clothes lighter and stronger.

Nylon, polyester, and acrylic are three different types of plastic used to make fibers.

plastics keep us safe

Some plastics are very strong and light. They are used to keep us safe. The **helmets** worn by cyclists and motor cyclists are made of a strong plastic that is not heavy to wear.

This helmet is made of plastic. It **protects** the bicyclist's head in an accident.

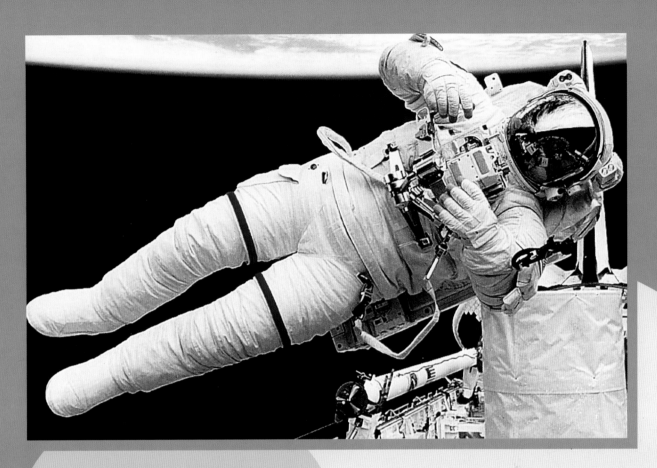

Space suits contain eight or nine layers of plastic materials. They protect the wearer from heat and cold.

Plastic sunglasses protect our eyes from the Sun's harmful rays.

Getting rid of waste plastic

Most plastics will not rot away. They will last for hundreds of years. Scientists are trying to make new plastic bags and wrappers that will rot away in time.

Plastic litter often gets washed up on the sea shore and has to be cleared up.

The easiest plastics to **recycle** are those that can be heated and made into new shapes.

These plastic bottles will be recycled and used to make fleece jackets.

Most plastics are made from oil. There is however only so much oil in the world, and we must use oil and plastics carefully. It is possible to reuse some kinds of plastic. This is called recycling.

Do it yourself

Looking at plastics

1 Collect some small
pieces of plastic.

2 How hard or soft are
your pieces of plastic?
Is it easy or difficult to
scratch them with a
metal nail?
(BE CAREFUL!)

3 Put your pieces of plastic in a bowl of water, one at a time. Which of the pieces float? Which of them sink?

4 Try to bend your pieces of plastic. Which bend easily? Which are hard to bend?

5 Which pieces of plastic can you see through?

Glossary

chemical One of the thousands of substances which make up all living things and the world around them.

conservatory A room with glass walls and roof.

copper A reddish-brown metal used for pipes, wires, coins, and some roofs.

dye A substance used to color other material.

electrician A person who works with electricity.

fiber A very thin thread.

helmet A strong covering to protect your head.

lead A soft, heavy, gray metal.

manufacture To make something with machines.

material Any substance from which things are made.

melt To make something into a liquid by heating it.

mold A container for making things that will set in the shape that is wanted.

plastic A strong, light substance that can be made into many different shapes.

polyethylene A light plastic used to make bags and wrappings.

polystyrene A soft kind of plastic used for packing or to keep things warm or cool.

protect To keep safe.

recycle To treat waste material so that it can be used again.

rot To go soft or bad so that the object is useless.

rust The red or brown substance that forms on iron or steel in damp air.

waterproof Something that keeps water out is said to be waterproof.

Index

Acrylic 23

Bakelite 9
Building with plastic 14-15

Cloth 22
Clothes 22-23
Coal 6
Conservatories 15, 30

Doors 14

Electricity 16, 17

Factory 6, 10
Fibers 22, 23, 30
Food 18-19, 20-21
Fuses 16

Helmets 24, 30

Litter 26

Metals 18
Molds 11, 12, 13

Nylon 23

Oil 6, 27

Pipes 14, 15, 18-19
Polyester 23
Polyethylene 9, 11, 20, 31
Polystyrene 9, 20, 21, 31

Recycling 26, 27, 31
Refrigerator 21
Rust 5, 31

Safety 24-25
Shaping plastic 10-11
Space suits 25
Sunglasses 25

Teflon 4
Tools 17
Toys 12-13
Types of plastic 8-9

Waste 26-27
Windows 14
Wood 6